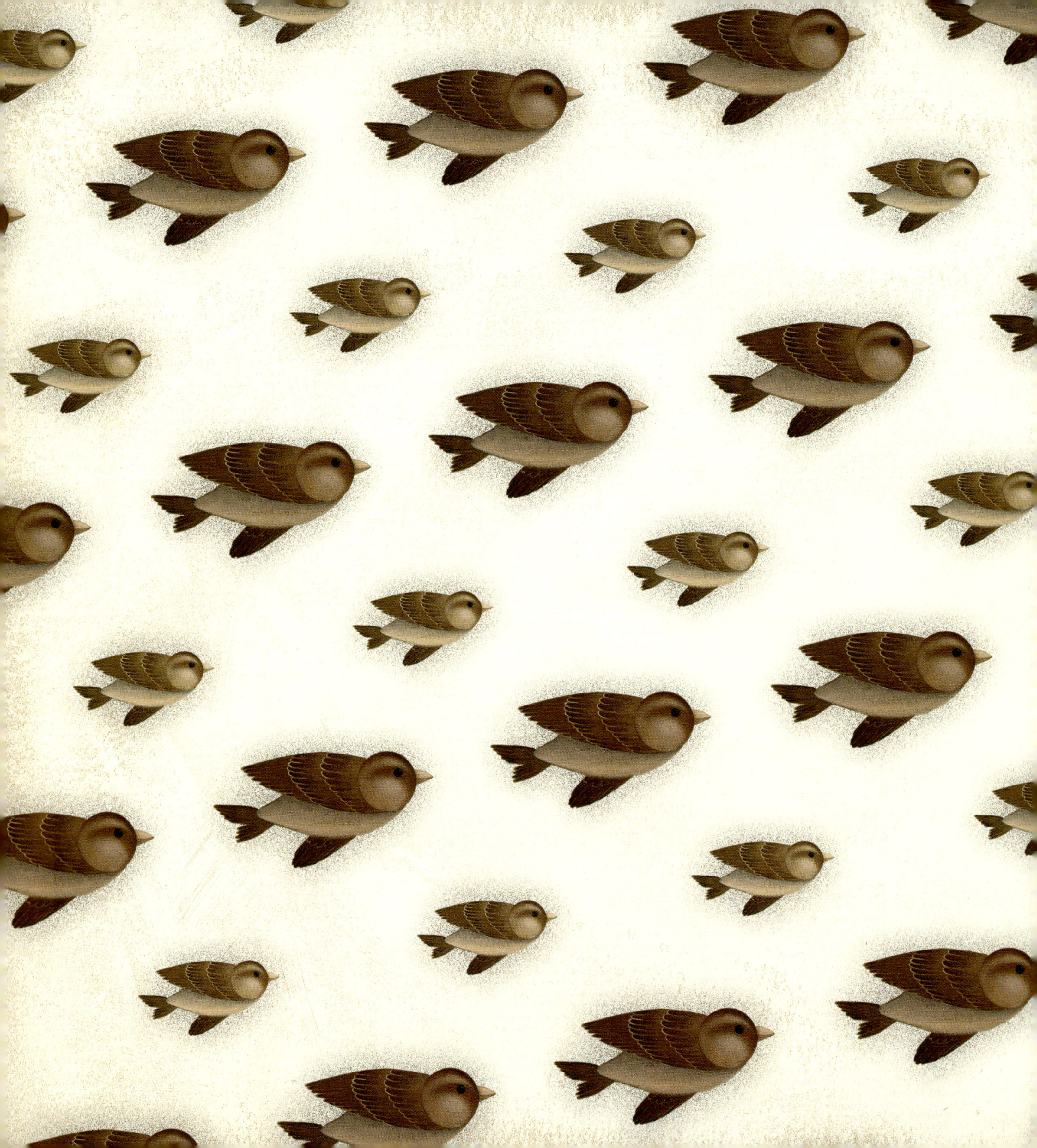

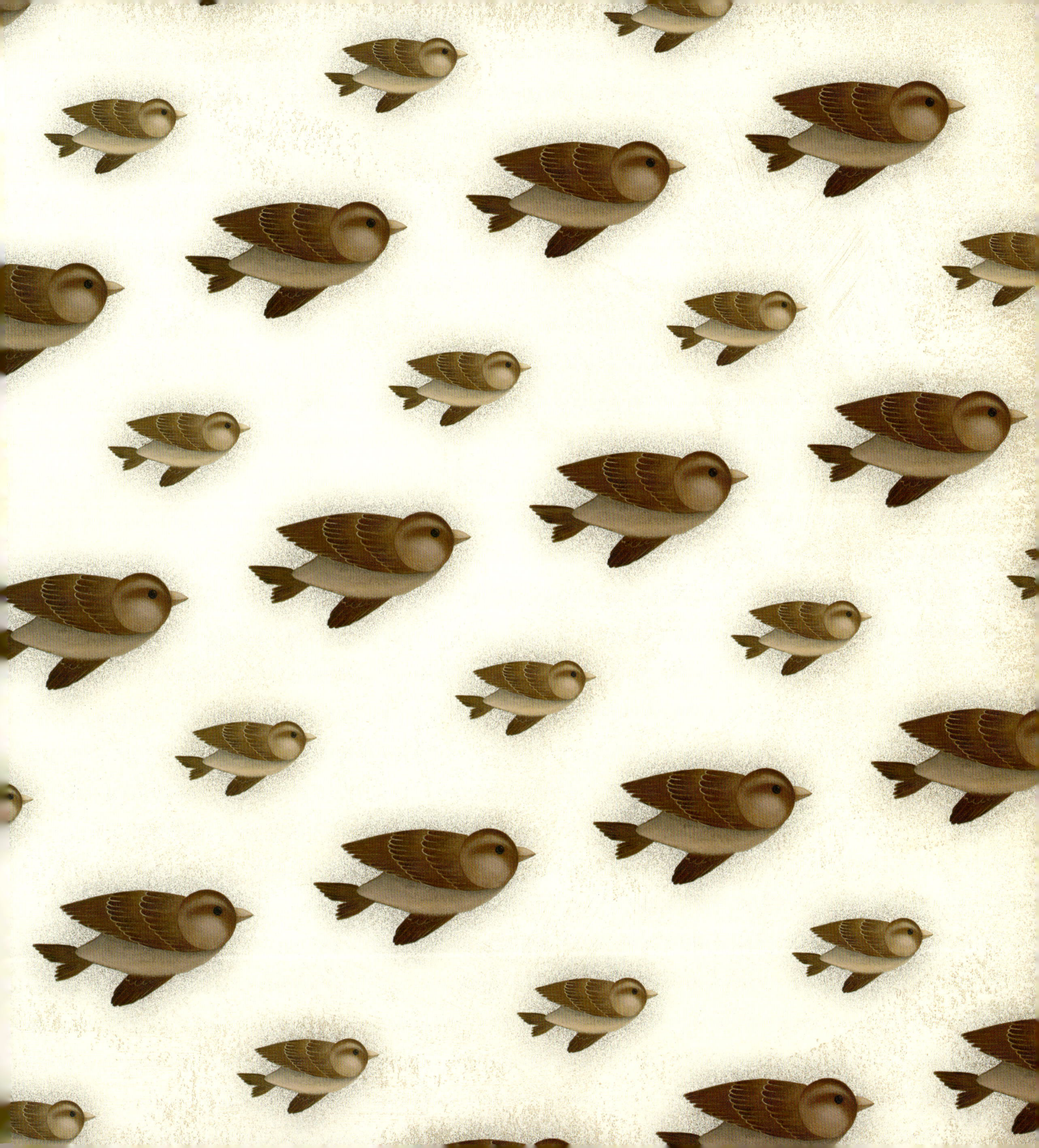

Sparrow Girl

WRITTEN BY
Sara Pennypacker

ILLUSTRATED BY
Yoko Tanaka

DISNEY · HYPERION BOOKS
NEW YORK

With many thanks to Lou Sheldon for sharing his memories,
and to Merryl Goldberg for connecting us
—SP

For Kimiyo and Paul, without whom I couldn't have started painting
—YT

Text © 2009 by Sara Pennypacker
Illustrations © 2009 by Yoko Tanaka

All rights reserved. Published by Hyperion Books for Children, an imprint of Disney Book Group. No part of this book may be reproduced or transmitted in any form or by any means, electronic or mechanical, including photocopying, recording, or by any information storage and retrieval system, without written permission from the publisher.
For information address Hyperion Books for Children,
114 Fifth Avenue, New York, New York 10011-5690.
First Edition · 1 3 5 7 9 10 8 6 4 2 · This book is set in Mrs Eaves Roman
Designed by Elizabeth H. Clark · Printed in Singapore
ISBN 978-1-4847-0722-7
F850-6835-5-13359

Visit www.hyperionbooksforchildren.com

There is a special providence in the fall of a sparrow.
Hamlet, Act 5, Scene 2

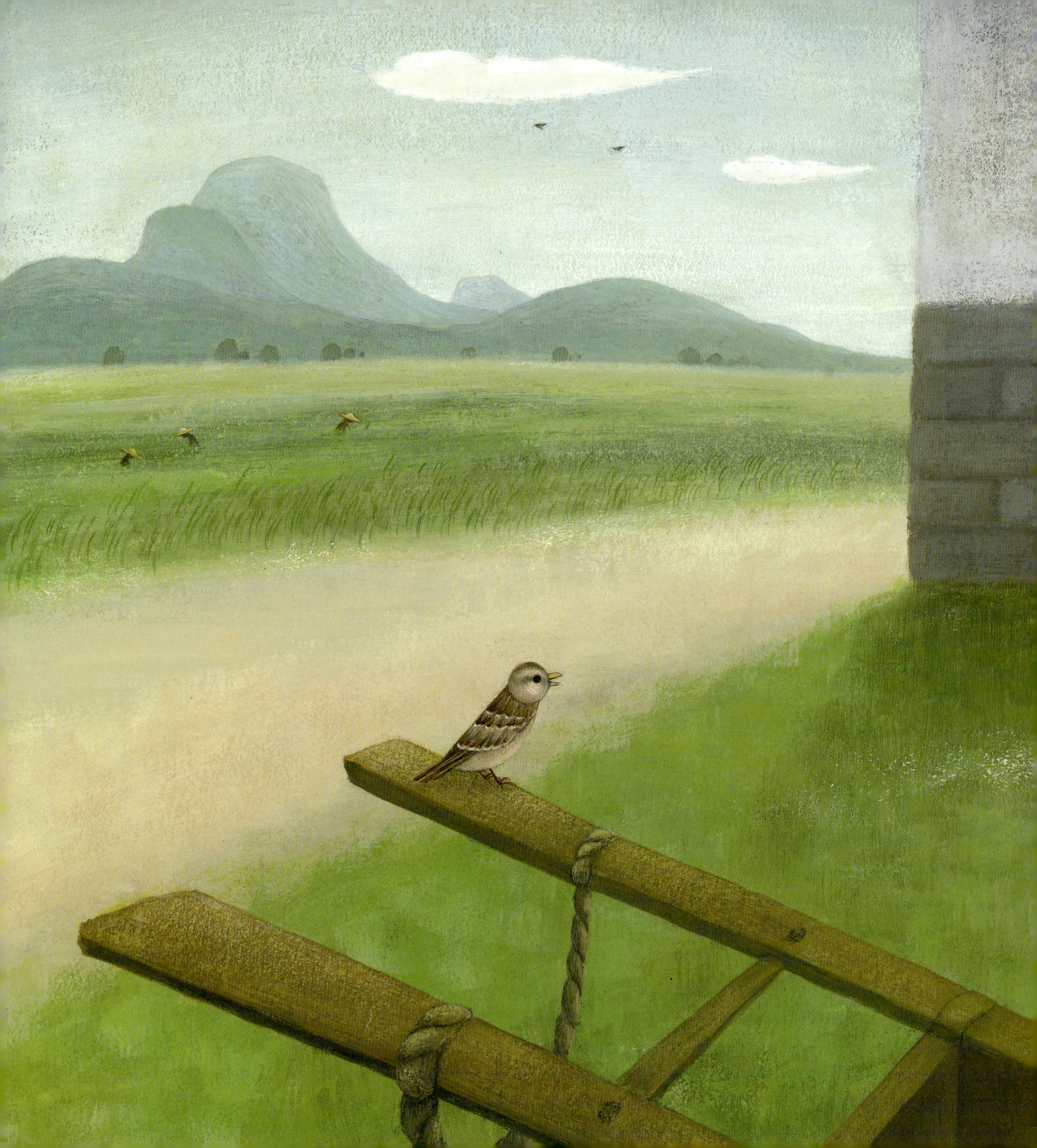

O NE DAY, NOT TOO LONG AGO, war was declared in China.

"Sparrows are our enemies! They eat too much grain. We must drive them from the land!" Older Brother held out the bag of firecrackers that Father had given him to help fight the war.

"I like sparrows," Ming-Li said quietly, walking home with Older Brother. She looked up and tried to imagine the sky empty, silent.

Mother and Father were talking about the plan, too. "The village barn is empty now. Next year it will be full of grain!"

"I could help you plant more seeds in the spring, Father," Ming-Li said. "And weed the fields, and . . ."

"You are not a farmer." Father patted her head. "You are only a small girl."

That night, Ming-Li couldn't sleep. Something bothered her, scratching at her thoughts like a monkey. She crept to Older Brother's sleeping mat.

"How will the other birds know?" she whispered, shaking his shoulder.

Older Brother rubbed his eyes and scowled in the moonlight.

"Won't our noise parade frighten the other birds, too? What if the nightingales fly away? Or the swallows, or . . . Pigeon?"

"Younger Sister, your brain is as small as a sparrow's!" hissed Older Brother. "Our Leader's plans are always perfect. They told us at school. Now, go to sleep!"

The next morning, a tremendous din woke Ming-Li. She ran to the window. A sea of people flooded the village, clanging gongs, crashing cymbals, beating drums, and shouting in their loudest voices. Firecrackers exploded like gunshots.

"Dress warmly," Mother said, handing her a rice cake. "You will be gone all day and into the evening."

Ming-Li and Older Brother picked up their pots and spoons, and went outside. The villagers were running through the streets, making so much noise the ground itself rumbled. They were looking up to search for enemy sparrows, but not down to see if they might trample a small girl.

Ming-Li clutched Older Brother's hand. He led her away from the thundering crowd and into the orchard.

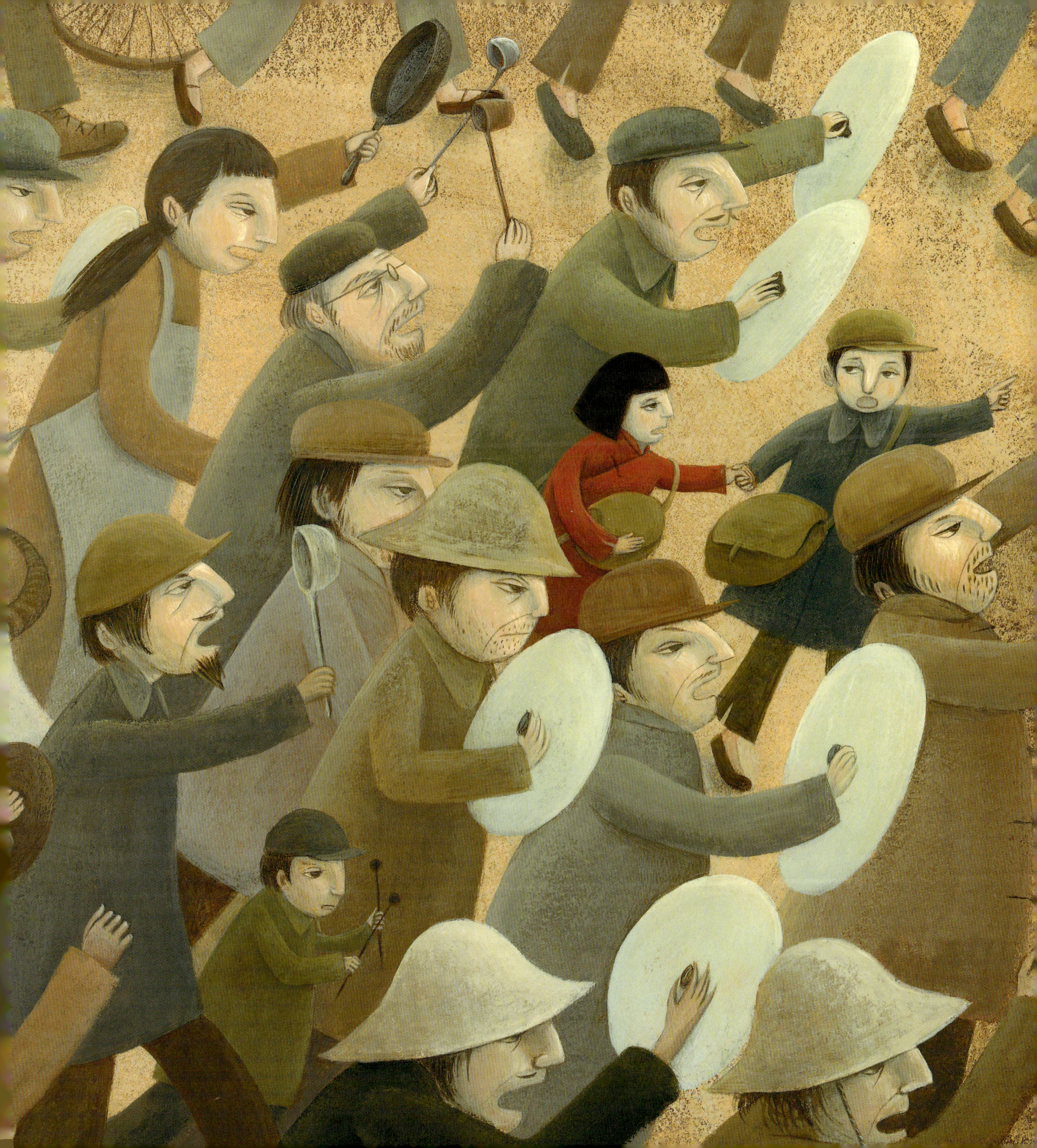

Older Brother stopped under a grove of apricot trees and lit a firecracker. *BOOM!* A cloud of sparrows rose and flew across to a row of pear trees. He followed and lit another firecracker beneath them.

Ming-Li clapped her hands over her ears and squeezed her eyes shut, but the firecrackers' loud, golden sparks were exploding inside her head now. She wanted to fly away, like a sparrow, to someplace high and safe.

Ming-Li set out for the road, but just as she reached it, she saw something fall from the sky like a stone. A group of villagers saw it too, and hurried over.

"It's been frightened to death!" Ming-Li cried. "We have to stop!"

"Dead sparrows don't eat grain!" crowed an old man beside her.

More birds fell to the ground, lifeless.

"*Ay—yi!* We're winning the Sparrow War!" cheered the others.

Ming-Li ran home. She climbed to the peak of the roof, to check on Pigeon. But his cage was empty—Older Brother must have sent his pet out yesterday.

Suddenly a plump silver bird flew toward her.

"You've come home!" Ming-Li held out her arm for Pigeon to land on. But he only fluttered in the air for a moment, and then fell with a soft thud on the curved clay tiles.

Pigeon lay limp and still except for his heart pounding beneath the pearly feathers of his breast. And then even that was still.

Tears filled Ming-Li's eyes. She tucked the bird into her jacket, climbed down from the roof, and set out for the orchards.

Older Brother was standing beneath a walnut tree, preparing to set off a firecracker. Ming-Li touched his elbow. "Wait."

Older Brother's face crumpled and his shoulders fell. He dropped his firecracker. Together they buried Pigeon under the walnut tree.

"The noise parade will kill all the sparrows in China. Maybe all the birds. We have to do something," Ming-Li said. "Will you help me?"

Older Brother nodded, his eyes red. "But no one can disobey Our Leader. What can we do?"

"Maybe some of the sparrows that fall to the ground are still alive, like Pigeon was. We could rescue them."

All that afternoon, whenever she saw a bird fall, Ming-Li hurried to the spot. Time after time, she was too late. But then, just as the lanterns were being lit, a small, brown bird dropped beside a quince bush, then fluttered up for a moment. Ming-Li's hope rose with it; she ran to the bush and found a sparrow struggling to its feet. She scooped the exhausted bird into her jacket.

"You're safe now, little friend," she whispered.

Around her, people were walking home, congratulating one another. "In two more days, there won't be a single sparrow left in all of China!"

Ming-Li wrapped her jacket more closely around her. She could feel the bird's tiny heart beating against her own. "Yes, there will," she promised.

She found Older Brother in the crowd. "Just one," she told him, letting him peek inside.

Together they brought the little sparrow to Pigeon's empty cage. Ming-Li filled the water cup and broke her rice cake into bits.

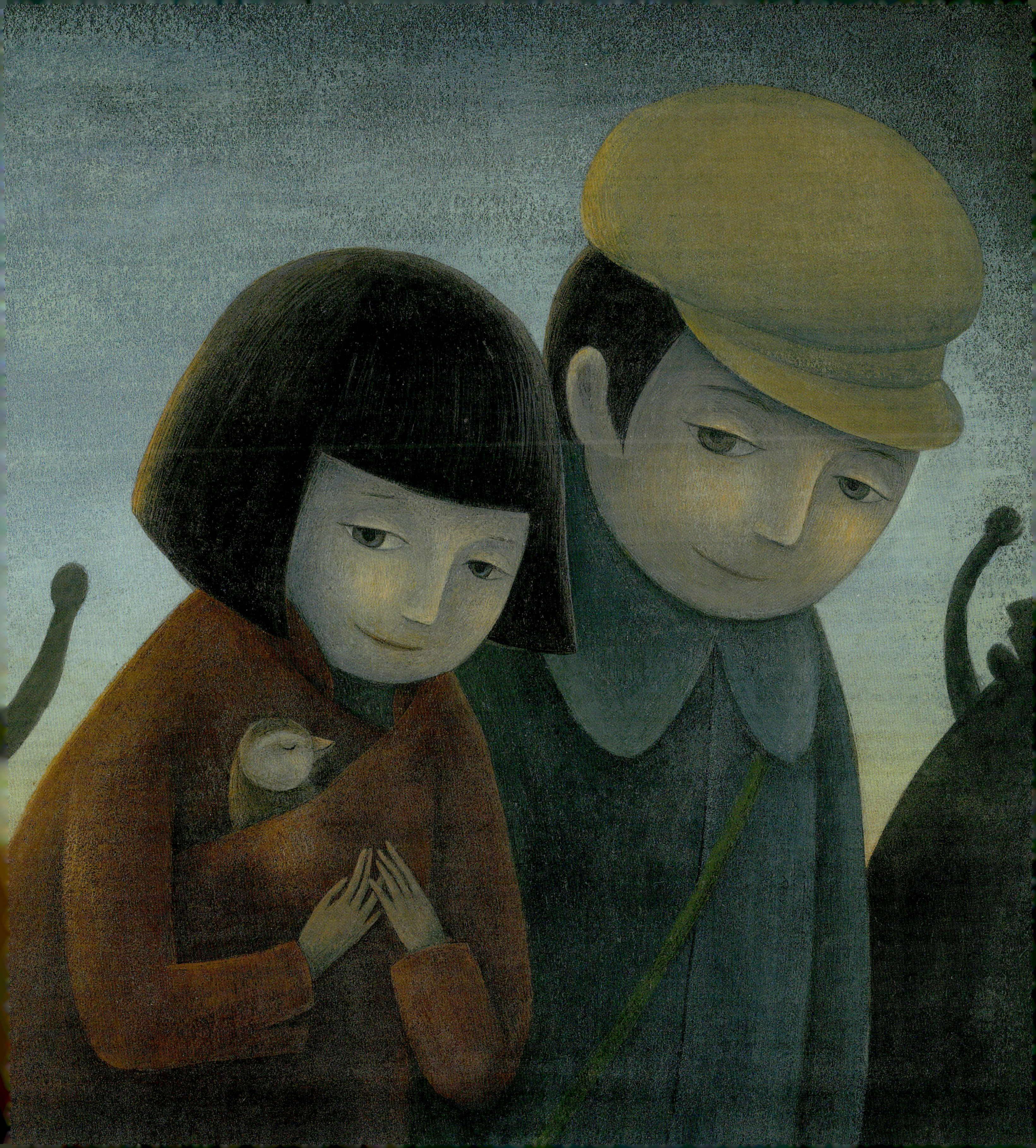

The next morning, she and Older Brother hurried out to search for birds to save. If any villagers were nearby when Ming-Li ran to a fallen sparrow, Older Brother distracted them. "Look! To the west! A flock of enemies!"

By afternoon, the birds were falling from the sky at a terrible rate.

"They're like raindrops," said Older Brother. "The sky is raining birds!"
"No," said Ming-Li. "They're like teardrops. The sky is crying birds."
By nightfall, they had rescued four more sparrows.

On the third day, the sky was nearly empty. Still the villagers poured through the streets, clanging gongs, clashing cymbals, beating drums, and shouting in their loudest voices. Ming-Li and Older Brother found only two more birds alive.

"Seven sparrows," said Ming-Li later looking into the cage on the rooftop. "When there used to be thousands."

"Seven sparrows," said Older Brother. "When there could have been none."

That night Ming-Li lay awake. Her sparrows would need room to fly soon. But if she let them loose, the villagers would hunt them.

The next morning she arose before dawn. She hurried to the rooftop, climbed down with the cage, and ran with it through the fields to the village barn. She released the birds inside. "Someday you'll fly under the sun again," she promised them.

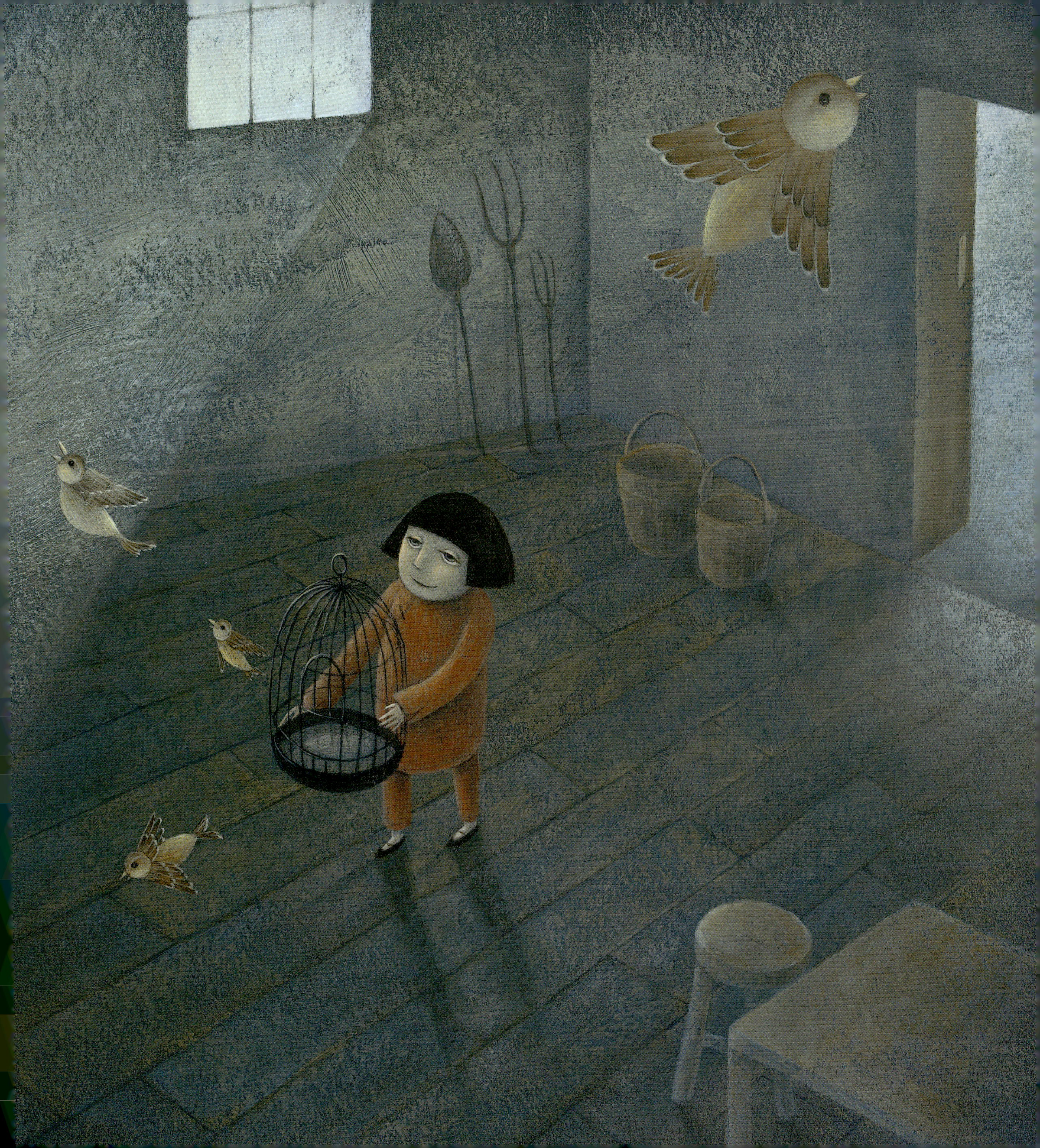

Each day after school, Ming-Li visited her sparrows. She watched them fly between the rafters, then swoop down to peck at worms and bugs.

But when spring came, Ming-Li worried. As soon as the first crop was harvested, the farmers would open up the barn. Where could she hide her sparrows then?

Already, Father and Older Brother had begun planting.

Ming-Li ached to go with them. "Let me help you," she begged each day.

"You are not a farmer." Her father smiled. "You are only a small girl."

One day in midsummer, Ming-Li noticed her father looked worried when he came back from the fields. "There is to be a meeting of all the farmers tomorrow," he said, "in front of the village barn."

The village barn! What if they went inside?

The next morning, Ming-Li followed her father. She hid beside the barn. The farmers sat in a circle, their faces serious.

"I will have no grain this year," said one. "The locusts are eating it all."

"The plums in my orchard are full of worms!" cried another.

"Weevils are eating my rice," added a third. "And grasshoppers are chewing through the bean stalks."

"There will be famine," said Ming-Li's father. "Our families will starve."

And then there was silence while the truth settled over them, cold and dark as a winter night.

Ming-Li couldn't help herself. She ran out from beside the barn. "It's because there are no sparrows! There are no sparrows to eat the insects now!"

"Ming-Li, go home!" cried her father.

But the eldest farmer held up his hand. "She is right," he said. "The sparrows were never our enemies."

"What does it matter?" asked the second farmer. "What's done is done."

Ming-Li whispered something in her father's ear. He stood. "Show us."

Ming-Li led the farmers to the barn and threw open the doors. She held her breath—how great would her punishment be?

Inside, the sparrows rose from the rafters and flew out into the fresh summer air. The farmers gasped in wonder. "Your daughter brings us a miracle!" they cried. "She brings us seven miracles!

"From this day, sparrows will be safe in our village. And we will tell everyone we meet from other villages about the wisdom of the Sparrow Girl."

"Yes," agreed Ming-Li's father. "My daughter is the Sparrow Girl. But she is something more. . . ."

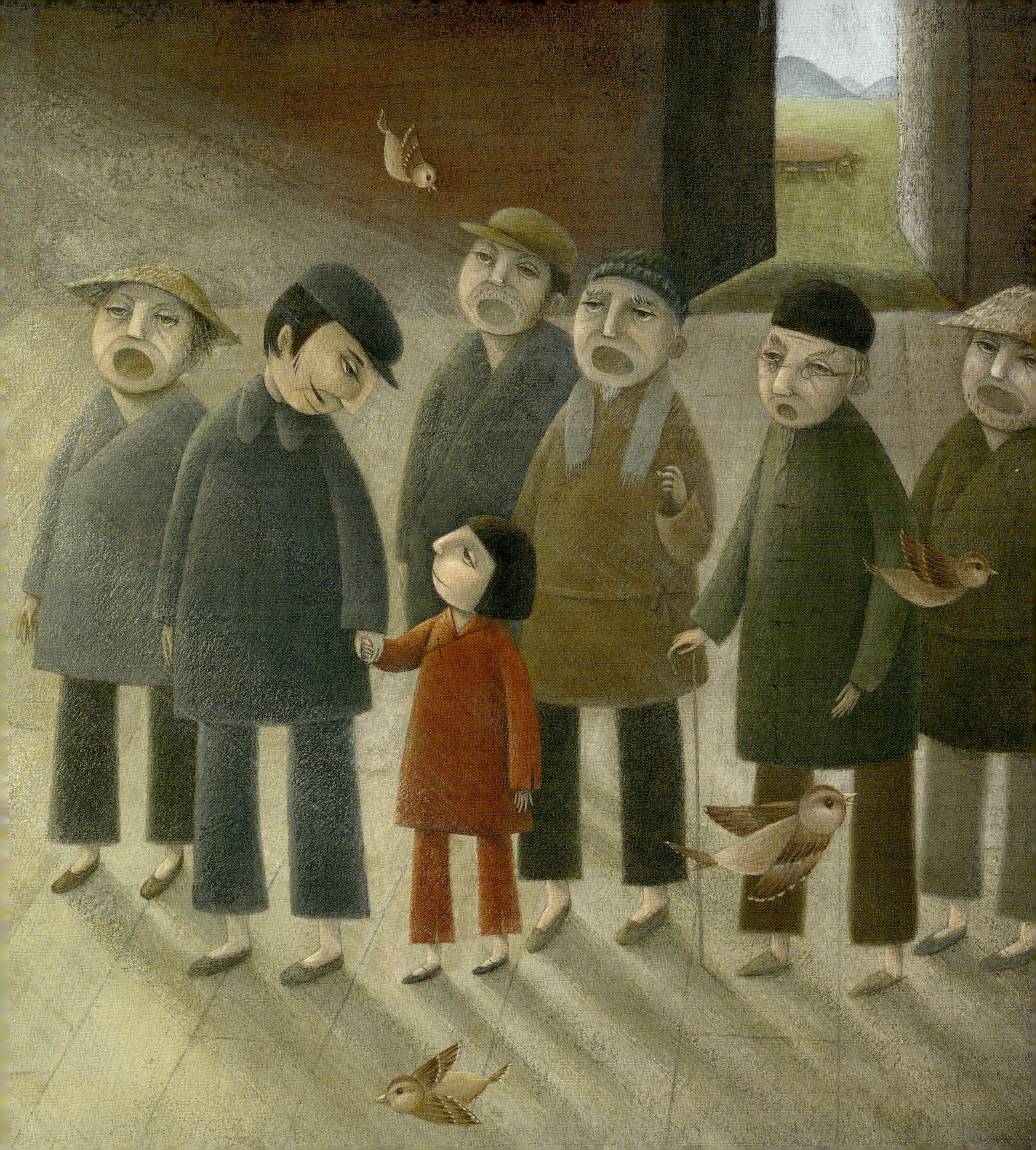

He lifted her to his shoulder. "Ming-Li is a true farmer."

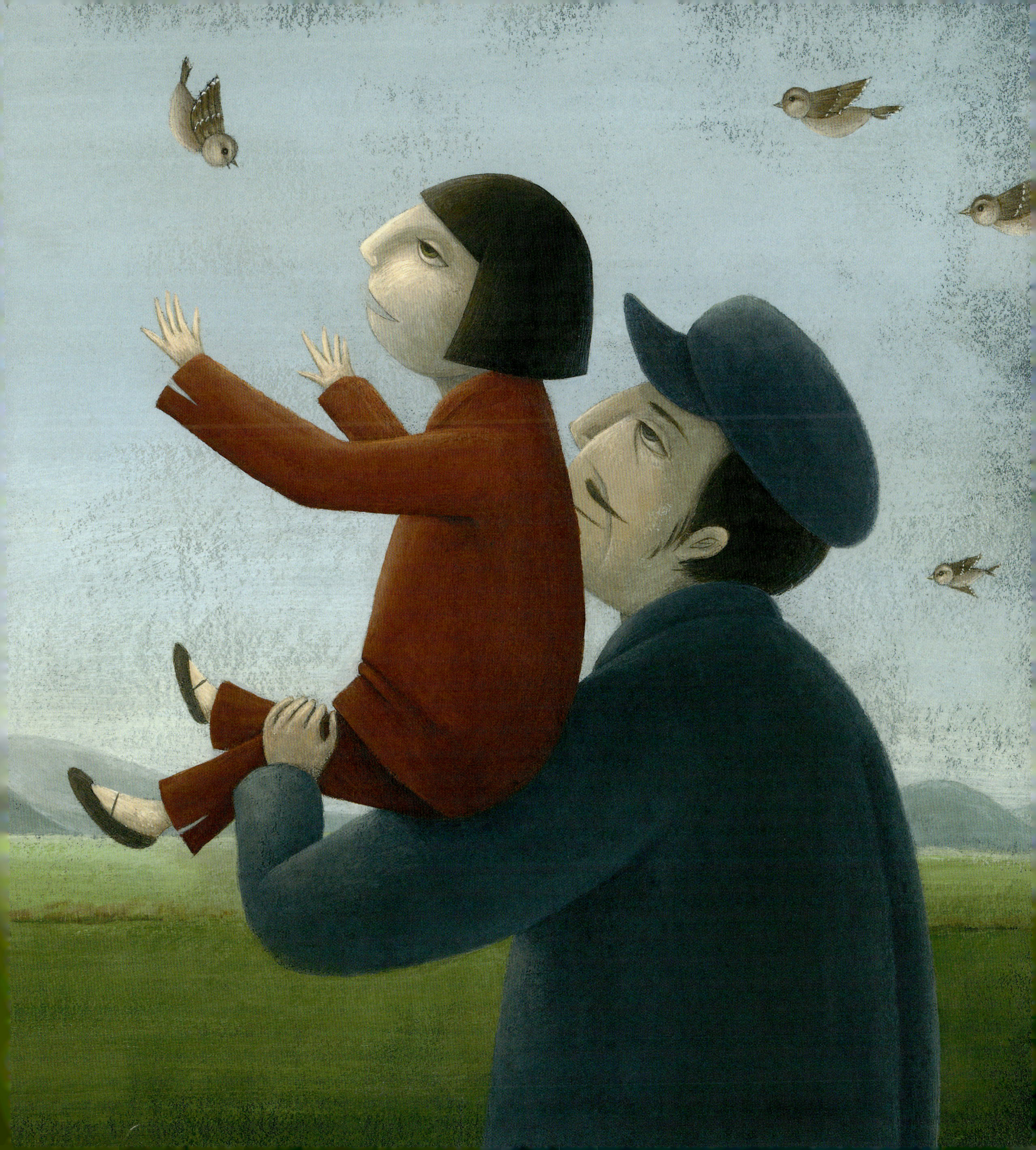

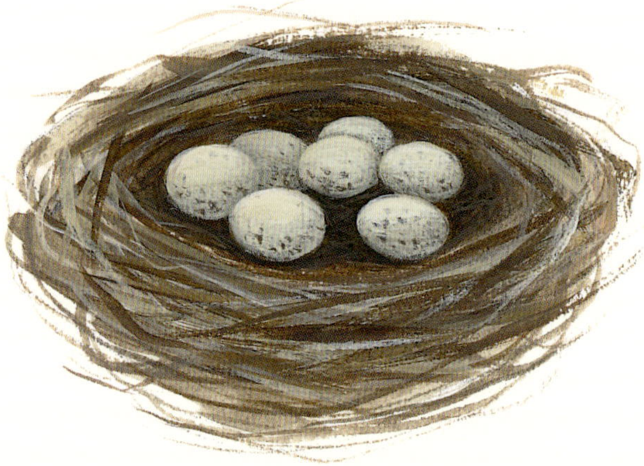

Author's Note

THE SPARROW WAR: In 1958, Chairman Mao Tse-Tung declared war on sparrows, blaming them for eating too much of China's wheat crop. His battle plan was simple: over a period of three days and evenings, all the able-bodied citizens in the country, including the schoolchildren, were to cover the land and make as much noise as possible so that the birds would die of exhaustion or heart attacks. The plan was effective—within three days the sparrow population was decimated—but deadly to humans: without the sparrows, the locust population grew to plague proportions, contributing to a famine that killed between thirty and forty million Chinese over the next three years.

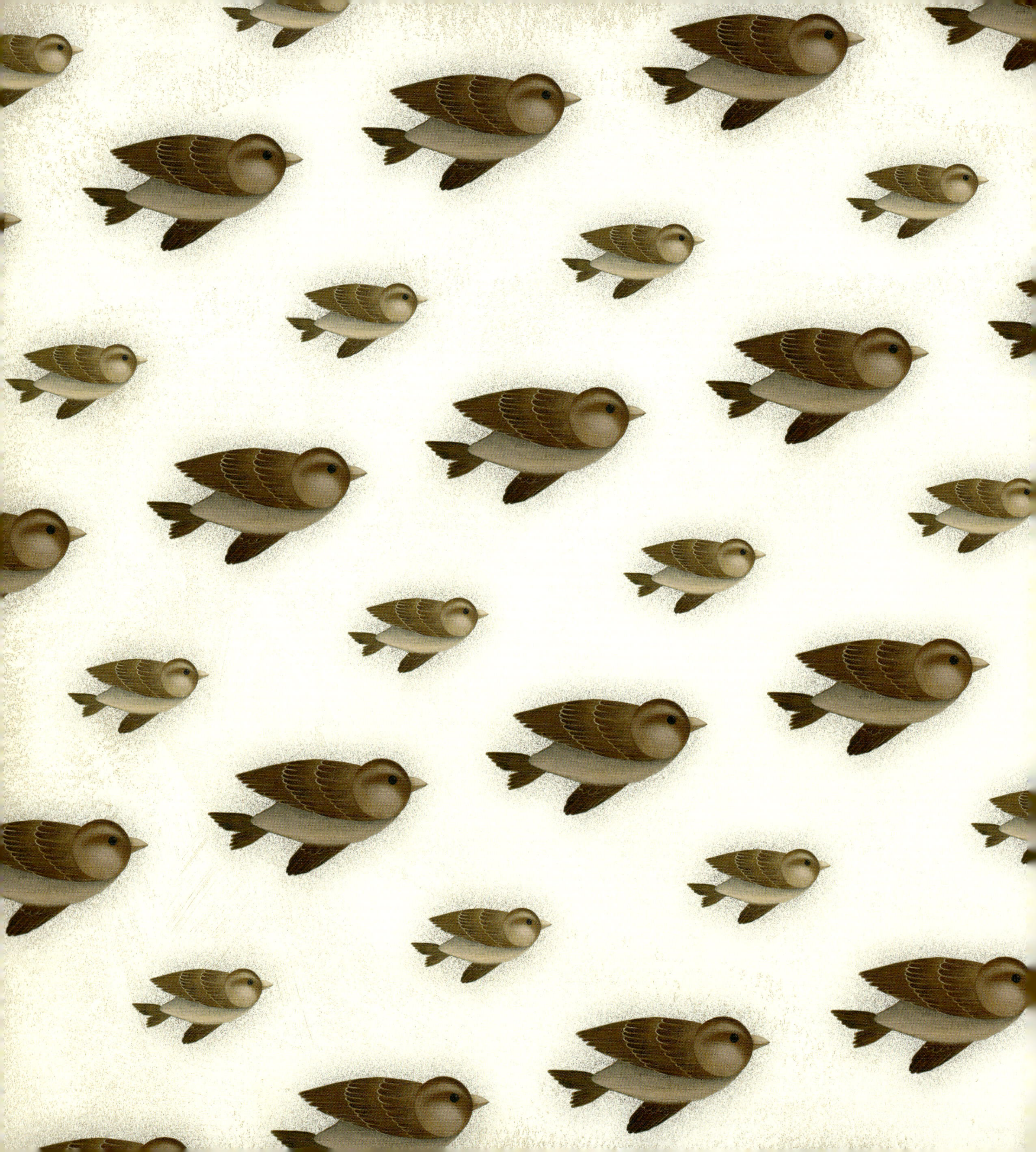

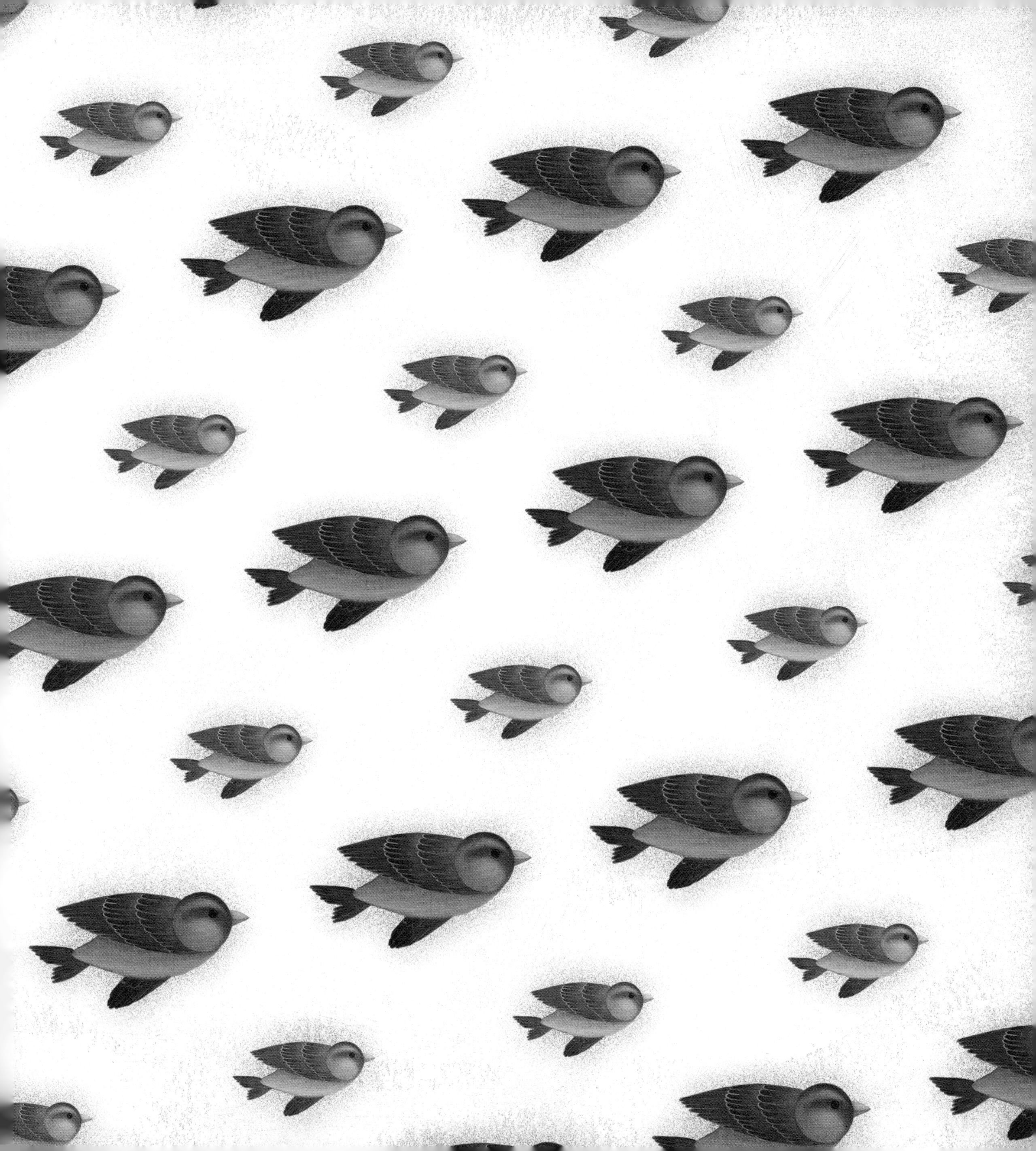